The Top 59 Reasons I vote Republican

Find out why God loves Republicans, and how Racism should affect our politicians.

by

Stuart M. Blessing

authorHOUSE

1663 Liberty Drive, Suite 200
Bloomington, Indiana 47403
(800) 839-8640
www.authorhouse.com

First published by AuthorHouse 05/14/04

ISBN: 1-4184-1978-8 (e)
ISBN: 1-4184-1977-X (sc)

Printed in the United States of America
Bloomington, Indiana

This book is printed on acid-free paper.

__Introduction__

I have been voting Republican my whole life, starting with Ronald Reagan. I have been confident in every vote and open with anyone who asked why I vote the way I do. As my children got older, they started to question me about my beliefs. When I watch political shows my children will ask me to explain what is being said. Some of our longest conversations have been after a State of the Union Speech.

Realizing my children were not the only ones who had these questions I put together this short book. Even though some of the topics we discuss could have entire books written about them, I have kept each explanation to a single page, trying to cover the fundamental truth of each.

I understand that not every Republican will agree with every position I take, and not every Democrat will disagree with every position I take. As you read through the book make a list of what you agree with and what you disagree with. If you agree with more than you disagree with, you probably should be voting Republican, too. I have also included a Test in the back of the book to help you determine whether you should be voting Republican or Democrat.

Thank you for taking the time to read my thoughts on some of the most provocative subjects in our society. I hope you receive benefit from the time you spend with this book.

God Bless

Table of Contents

Because 2 Plus 2 is Always 4... 1

Because Abraham Lincoln is a Republican 2

Because Arnold Schwarzenegger is a R.i.N.O............................. 3

Because Barbara Boxer is a Democrat... 4

Because Big Business is Good.. 5

Because Bill Clinton is a Democrat... 7

Because George W. Bush is a Republican 8

Because God Bless America 9

Because God loves Republicans 10

Because Hillary Clinton is a Democrat...................................... 11

Because I Believe in a Woman's Right to Choose..................... 12

Because I Believe Old Story 14

Because I like Cowboys 15

Because Illegal Aliens are Illegal... 16

Because J.F.K. was right 18

Because Liberals Want to Follow Europe................................... 19

Because Living in Captivity Destroys the Spirit 20

Because Martin Luther King Jr. was Right................................. 22

Because Nancy Pelosi is a Democrat.. 23

Because of Adam in the Garden of Eden 24

Because of Charity.. 25

Because of Communism 27

Because of Criminals 28

Because of Diversity 29

Because of Evil 31

Because of Gun Control... 32

Because of Liberty 33

Because of Marriage 34

Because of Maturity... 35

Because of National Security... 36

Because of our Rights 37

Because of Pornography 38

Because of Racism... 39

Because of Rich People 41

Because of Stupidity 43

Because of Taxes... 44

Because of the Bill of Rights 46

Because of the Death Penalty 47

Because of the Democrats Sales Strategy 48

Because of the Economy.. 49

Because of the Family Farm 51

Because of the Golden Rule... 53

Because of the Main Stream 55

Because of the Minimum Wage 57

Because of the Pledge of Allegiance... 59

Because of the Right-Wing Conspiracy.. 60

Because of the Special Interests Groups....................................... 61

Because of Tolerance 63

Because of World Peace... 65

Because Religious People Cannot Vote for Democrats. 67

Because Small Business is Good 68

Because the Democrats are on the Wrong Side of Good and Bad
.... 69

Because the Democrat Leaders will turn the war in Iraq in to
Vietnam. 70

Because the Devil is Working Hard in America. 72

Because the Liberal Media Misquotes God 73

Because There is a Right and Proper way to live Your Life 74

Because Tom Daschle is a Democrat... 76

Because our Children Deserve the Best.. 77

The Voters Test.. 78

Because 2 Plus 2 is Always 4

There is right and wrong in this world and they are constant, just like we have physical laws, such as gravity. Some people claim the way they choose to live their lives cannot be wrong. If it works for them, then it should be acceptable to everyone. Basically saying that there is no right or wrong, as long as you are not hurting anyone, whatever you choose for yourself is ok.

Right is always right, and wrong is always wrong, just as 2+2 is always 4. You cannot have relative morality; either your actions are moral or they're not. Morality is not what your neighbor says is acceptable behavior. Morality has been based on the laws set forth in the Old Testament of the Bible. The Ten Commandments are the first record of laws on how man should behave. Every king in every kingdom had set up rules but nothing like the Ten Commandments. Six out of the Ten concern how men should behave towards each other. "Honor your father and mother, you shall not commit murder, you shall not commit adultery, you shall not steal, you shall not give false testimony, you shall not covet your neighbor's house, wife, servants or anything that belongs to him."

For Christians and Jews this is very simple, God said it, its right. Many people in the world believe if there is not a law currently on the books about it, they can do what ever they want and it's ok.

Remember what is legal is determined by the government of man. What is Moral has been set forth by God. The laws of man will change depending on which ones are in charge but morality will never change. Just like gravity and 2+2 they are constant. Nothing that is immoral can be right and nothing that is moral can be wrong.

Because Abraham Lincoln is a Republican

President Lincoln is the foundation of the modern day Republican Party. His absolute belief in the ideals of this country's being conceived in liberty and dedicated to the proposition that all men were created equal stands to day.

Equality under the law allows everyone to succeed to the complete level of his or her God-given talent and determination. Equality under the law does not mean everyone gets five. Fair does not mean that if they have five I should get five, even if I only earned one. Liberty means freedom to live unobstructed by the government, to earn what you will and to be in control of your own destiny.

President Lincoln worked hard to go from his small log cabin in Illinois to the White House. He suffered many failures and never quit. He was driven by the idea of always doing the right thing even if the right thing was the hard thing to do.

His life stands as a living monument to our country, the ideals of personal responsibility and determination of living life by his beliefs.

Because Arnold Schwarzenegger is a R.i.N.O.

Ri.N.O. Stands for Republican in Name Only, meaning they do not maintain the core values of the Republican Party. There are no requirements in order to register as a Republican. Anyone can say, "I am a Republican". Republicans are a little more particular about which politicians call themselves Republican than are most other political parties. The foundation of the Republican Party is conservationism; if a registered Republican does not endorse conservative values, they are not fully representative of the party. That is where Schwarzenegger is; he supports conservative financial values and fiscal policy but is a social Liberal.

I could not vote for Schwarzenegger, even if he was the best chance to get a Republican in the Governor's seat. I disagree with individuals who will surrender their social and religious beliefs in order to get the fiscal polices they want. My social positions are biased on morality taught by my faith and the laws of God about how we should conduct ourselves on earth. People who will sell their beliefs to get the budget under control should be ashamed.

I vote for Conservatives, Conservatives are mostly registered Republican. That is why I vote for Republicans.

Because Barbara Boxer is a Democrat

Not only do I disagree with Ms. Boxer politically, but also I saw her stand Side-by-side with Gray Davis after he pulled California down to new depths. The liberal economic tax-and-spend plan drove businesses out of the state and the deficit to over 18 billion dollars. The tax burden placed on Californians was so heavy they were being crushed. What was the answer Gray Davis had? He tripled the car tax. Spending completely out of control with a promise to spend more. Yet there stood Barbara Boxer next to Gray Davis giving her full support to him and his failed leadership.

It is said that you can tell a lot about a person by who their friends are. Well, Gray Davis is gone; Californians should send Ms. Boxer with him.

Because Big Business is Good

Yes, I said big business is good. I know you keep hearing about how bad big business is. Big Oil, Big Finance, Big Telecommunications and Microsoft. Wal-Mart is taking over and Clear Carmel Communication owns too many TV and radio stations.

Big business drives the economy; the economy is totally at the mercy of the stock exchange. You will never hear a stock analyst complaining about how a small business is doing and how it will hurt the market.

Big business offers the best benefits: 401k plans with the company putting in matching funds. They pay 50% to 90% of the employee's health care and offer long-term employment opportunities with pension plans.

Big business has great buying power so it can keep costs down and sell its products and services for less.

Big business employs about 50% of the non-governmental employees in this country.

Unions love big business, you never hear about Sissy's Hair Hut voting on going union. The unions are only interested in dealing with big business or total industries if they can control all of the small companies doing business.

Big business pays a tremendous amount of taxes, federally as well as to the state and local governments.

With all this being true, why do the democratic politicians always complain about big business? So they can make people feel small and in need of help. When people need help they need someone to go to, and surprise, surprise, there is the politician waiting to offer their help.

Don't fall into the trap.

Because Bill Clinton is a Democrat

I know, I know, to some of you he is a hero.

But, would you trust him with your daughter?

Would you like him to mentor your son?

If the answers are no, you understand why you shouldn't trust him with anything else.

If the answers are yes, then you will get what you deserve. Congratulations.

Because George W. Bush is a Republican

What a tremendous leader he has been. He leads this country and the world fearlessly; he steps out first with the boldness of a lion. When fear strikes the hearts of the leaders across the world, he stands firm on his convictions. He invites all to join him, yet will not be deterred from the straight and narrow.

I do not agree with everything he has done, the growth of government concerns me, but I completely respect him as a president and as a man. What a change from the previous eight years, when I was embarrassed of who we had elected as our president.

I believe 100 years from now, historians will place George W. Bush among the top five or ten most successful Presidents in U. S. history.

<u>Because God Bless America</u>

Should never be removed from our lips, our walls, our schools, our courts or our White House.

In the first draft of the Declaration of Independence, the beginning was: ***We The People of God.***

Most of our founding fathers believed in the providence of God and in His provision for the future. Let's not use the excuse "every body does not believe in God" to remove His blessings from this country. Let's face it, not everyone believes in "The Theory of Evolution" but we all have to learn about it in school.

Remember, We The People of God have the constitutional right to freedom of religion. You do not have the constitutional right to freedom from religion.

God Bless America

Because God loves Republicans

Yes God loves Republicans who are His children and are mostly Christians. Republicans are for the displaying of the 10 Commandments, for praying in schools, for "in God we trust," against abortion, and if you can back up your argument with Biblical truth, a Republican is more likely than not to agree with you.

On the other hand, you have Democrats, Independents and several other varieties of political views. How does God feel about all of them? If they are encouraging young girls to have abortions, they tell people that homosexuality is a legitimate alternative lifestyle and fight against praying in schools. They will not allow the 10 Commandments to be displayed in schools, courts or any state or federal building. Also fight against any nativity scene in a town square. Basically denying God access to our lives outside of the church walls.

How does God feel about them? He loves them with all his heart. God is love, He is forgiveness. Some uninformed people will tell you that God hates the sinner. That could not be further from the truth, He loves every single person who has ever lived on this earth. God, like any Father, does not always like what we do, and yes, He will allow you to reap what you sow, but that is not out of hate. Just like when I discipline my children whom I love, I do it because I love them and want them to do the right things in life so that life will go well for them.

You may hate God, but He loves you no matter what. He does want you to follow the rules so that life will go well for you.

Because Hillary Clinton is a Democrat

I should not have to explain it.

Because I Believe in a Woman's Right to Choose.

1 She can choose if she is going to become sexually active....

or not.

#2 If she chooses to become sexually active she has the right to choose if she will take some form of protection from becoming pregnant. She has many forms of birth control that are very reliable.

#3 If she chooses to become sexually active she has the right to choose with whom she does and does not have sex.

#4 She has the right to choose whether the man she has consented to have sex with uses birth control or not.

After she makes all of her choices she then becomes pregnant. She made that choice. She chose to become pregnant by not preventing the natural result of having sex. It is no secret to anyone over the age of twelve how you become pregnant.

Now the hard part: if she has made bad choices she does not have the right to kill her unborn baby. She does have the right to make the father financially responsible for the baby. But the idea of killing the baby because she made bad choices is totally repugnant to any man or woman with a conscience.

I believe most people would accept if a woman's choices have been taken away from her through rape or incest. She needs to have some recourse under the law. Or if her life is in jeopardy from carrying the baby to term, she should have the right under the law to choose whether she is willing to risk her life to save the baby's life.

Understand that ending a baby's life should be a last resort, not considered another medical procedure, like having a wart removed or even cancer surgery. Remember, in every abortion somebody dies.

Because I Believe Old Story

You know the one, you give a man a fish you feed him for a day, but if you teach a man to fish you feed him for a lifetime.

If we all can agree on this, why then do we not do it?

In the United States we have what are called entitlement programs. We feed, clothe, house, provide medical care and prescription drugs for people who will not do it for themselves.

First, why are they entitled to have everyone else pay for them? I don't know. The only reason I can come up with is because we care. I care, don't you? Then let's really help them by teaching them how to fish.

If we stop the entitlement attitude and have the expectation that every able-bodied member of our country will contribute; even if their contribution is just to pay for themselves, we can end poverty in a single generation.

That's a bold statement, but true. Here is how it will work. Children who see their parents go to work in order to take care of the family learn that's how the world works. Children who see their parents sit home and receive free money, housing, food and medical, learn that's how it works.

If we, as a united country, make the investment to teach everyone how to take care of themselves, they will teach their children to do the same. The children will know what is expected from them and will meet the expectations.

Because I like Cowboys

Cowboys are trustworthy, strong, hardworking, truthful and dependable. If a cowboy tells you something, you can count on it. You may like what they say; you may not like what they say. But you can be guaranteed that they will do what they say. Make no mistake, a cowboy will tell you what they think with no bull. They do not talk out of both sides of their mouth.

Every one living west of the Mississippi River owes the cowboys and people like them a debt of gratitude. Their ability to tame the West opened this country to average families.

The opponents of President Bush call him a cowboy as if it's a bad thing. I like having a man who possesses the attributes of a cowboy in the Oval Office. How about you?

<u>Because Illegal Aliens are Illegal</u>

I don't know where it started, but there is a movement in this country to give people who have come to this country illegally all of the benefits of being an American. They are not Americans; they are not entitled to the benefit of the services that our taxes pay for.

We pay a very high level of taxes in this country, so that we can have the best services available. When people come here and use up our money, they are stealing from our children and us. We are going into debt in this country paying for schools, doctors and social services for people who are not members of our American Family.

If someone comes across our borders, finds you and steals your wallet with $100.00 in it, you would expect the police to arrest them and either put them in jail or send them back to where they belong. They stole from you and you have the right to be upset. Why is it different when what they steal is your tax money? They drain the money out of our school systems in California, Arizona, Texas, New Mexico, Florida and more. We spend over $7 billion a year educating illegal aliens. That's your tax money; that money should be spent on your children. You should be upset when someone steals from your children.

If we give illegal aliens a valid drivers license, we make them legitimate residents. They can even vote; the most precious right we have is the right to decide who runs the country. When illegal aliens come into this country breaking our laws they should not have that right. They could put someone who you disagree with in office. If American citizen commits a felony, one of the punishments is they lose the right to vote.

If we set laws to protect ourselves, we must enforce them in order to be safe. We must be able to do background checks, health screenings and determine whether the people who are coming in will be productive members of our country or not.

Because J.F.K. was right

When he proclaimed, "Ask not what your county can do for you but what you can do for your country".

That is how we should all live every day. If everyone who has something to offer would live the life God gave them with an attitude of service to others, every need would be met.

The Democratic politicians make life about what the government can do for you, if you just vote for them. Give them the power they want, and they will give you a program to meet whatever needs they say you have.

We do not need any more programs, we need opportunity: the opportunity to go to work and raise our families without the politicians invading our lives. The opportunity to send our children to a good school where the teachers can pass or fail children based on their test scores and class work, not on the government programs that say all children must move up so we don't hurt their feelings. The opportunity to save some of the money we earn instead of the government taking it so they can pay for more programs.

Let's all stop asking what the government can do for us and start doing for ourselves.

Because Liberals Want to Follow Europe

Liberals like the example the Europeans set: the socialistic godless society they live in. Liberals like the fact that many European countries will not make an international move without the approval of the United Nations. They like the relaxed attitude towards sexuality, nudity, and physical freedom.

First of all, Americans are leaders, not followers. I do not advocate following anyone, especially a continent we had to save twice. Secondly, our country was founded on Biblical principles of personal responsibility and morality. I believe that is the main reason the United States is the best place in the world to live. Also, we can never put decisions for our national security in the hands of anyone but our elected officials. It's said that Americans are uptight about sex. Just because we do not have topless beaches does not mean we are uptight. We have relaxed to an almost ridiculous level. Have you seen a movie lately? Try a PG 13 movie; who is it that decided 13-year-old boys and girls should see naked women and a high level of sexuality? I have been embarrassed on several occasions when I brought home a movie I thought would be family appropriate, only to be surprised by a pair of bare breasts. That was not what I was expecting in a movie that was rated for 13 year olds.

When I look at Europe, I see nothing we as a county should emulate. The United States of America is a leader, not a follower. We should not look to countries like France for clues on running a country. We should look to the values of limited government and personal responsibility we were founded on. The idea of God-based morality will continue to work well for everyone who tries it.

Because Living in Captivity Destroys the Spirit

When one of the greatest beasts God ever created is taken out of the jungle or off the plains of Africa and put in a zoo, it is no longer the King of the Jungle. This lion will walk around its cage and maintain total control over his new small world. And for a time he will look for a way to get out and escape his confinement. The Zookeepers have created an environment that resembles the land the lion was taken from to give the lion a sense that he belongs there. Some well-meaning people would say what a good life this lion has now. We feed him; we have built a nice home for him. It's not the wide-open lands of Africa but the lion should have a good life. He does not have to hunt for his food or fight off other lions to keep his pride. We've given him everything he needs to be happy. We should be proud of ourselves. When new cubs are born they never know anything but the cage they were born in. They will never learn how to hunt on the open plains of Africa. They will never have the chance to fight for a pride of their own. And worst of all, we can never send them back. They would not know how to hunt or where to go for food, water, shelter, or how to take care of their young. By providing all of the lion's needs we have permanently confined them to relying on their masters for survival. Without their masters they would DIE. This is the same policy our Democratic politicians have used to wipe out poverty. We built big zoos for poor people to live in: "the Projects." We give them food stamps so they can eat without having to hunt.

We give them a check every month so they can have the basic comforts of life. We give them free health care so that when they get sick we will take care of them. All of this, and the zookeepers do not require the recipients to work for any of it. We do have some requirements such as if you are young mother and want to get the government to take care of you. The baby's father cannot live in the home. Forget about getting married to the baby's father, you will loose every benefit we give you right then. On the other hand, if you have more children, we as a society will give you more money. The program is set up so that those held in this captivity are trapped by fear. Any attempt to get themselves out of the zoo comes with a big short-term price. Our captives for the most part do not have any marketable skills. So if they make the very difficult decision to get out of the zoo, they will start at the bottom rung of the corporate ladder. Most companies will hire people with no skills if they have a good attitude and appearance. Communication skills go a long way toward getting any job. When a company hires someone without skills they understand it is the company's responsibility to train them to do the job they were hired to do. But the starting point does not pay much and may be part- time with no benefits, or the benefits like health care may cost so much they cannot afford them. For men and women trapped in this position they look at the choices they have and soon find out that it pays more not to leave the zoo. Very many of them decide that they can be happy living under the rules of captivity because nothing is required of them. Our attempt to wipe out poverty has created two new generations of families who do not have the skills to survive in the jungle.

The cost of our current policy towards poverty needs to be measured in more than money. It needs to be measured in the lives that are being destroyed. Why are we not providing job training? Why do we not teach them how to hunt and how to survive in the jungle? Politics, somehow it has become politically incorrect to expect people to assume responsibility for their own lives. It is appropriate for the strong to help the weak; it is appropriate for the rich to help the poor. The help that is provided needs to help people help themselves for a lifetime. Let's not make them dependent; let's help them become independent.

Because Martin Luther King Jr. was Right

He was right when he told us to judge each other by the content of our character, not the color of our skin.

Because Nancy Pelosi is a Democrat

I have listened to Ms. Pelosi over the years and have never agreed with anything that she has ever said.

I do not always agree with every Republican on every issue, but I always disagree with Ms. Pelosi. If ever I am unsure of what my position should be. I find out what Ms. Pelosi says about the issue and do the opposite. This is a sure-fire way to be right every time.

Because of Adam in the Garden of Eden

In Genesis chapter 2 verse 15, *"The Lord God took the man and put him in the Garden of Eden to work it and take care of it "* The Garden of Eden was perfect, no weeds, thorns, thistles or bad bugs. So what work would there be for Adam to do? Prune; trim, thin out to prevent overgrowth. That's right that is how you take care of the garden. Have you ever seen someone tend to a Rose Garden? It's hard work; the pruning must be done precisely. The proper pruning allows the rose bush to grow well and to produce the best flowers possible.

If the Garden of Eden needed a man to tend to it, why would anyone believe our National Forests would not need the same? The Democratic Party is beholden to the environmentalists who hate logging or any other interference of nature. Therefore, the Democratic politicians oppose governmental management of our forests. They do not want to allow thinning of the trees and brush. Somehow they think that by leaving the forests alone they will tend themselves. God put in a natural thinning program; it's called a forest fire. Lightning strikes start them, and stopping one is next to impossible without the help of the natural forest fire extinguishers: rain and cold. We spend a lot of money fighting forest fires and loosing.

We need to tend to the garden God put us in, each part in its own way. The forest-thinning idea will reduce the risk of fire and allow the government to sell the trees in order to pay the bill for taking care of our countries' largest natural resource.

Because of Charity

The top ten most generous states in charitable giving voted for George W. Bush in 2000.

The bottom ten, or least generous states voted for Al Gore in 2000.

This is very interesting information. Why would conservatives be more generous than liberals? No, it's not because they have more money, two of the Al Gore states were California and New York, two of the richest states in the country. Is it because conservatives are more compassionate than liberals? No, I don't think so.

Let me submit my hypothesis.

Conservatives believe that it is not the government's responsibility to meet all the needs of every individual. It is the individual's responsibility to provide for themselves and their family. It is also the church's responsibility to help those who are down on their luck. They believe in helping a friend move, fix a car, mow the lawn or get a ride to the doctor or home from the auto repair shop. They believe in giving food to the local food bank because they are part of the community, and it is the responsibility of every good member of the community to help out.

Liberals believe that it is the responsibility of the government to meet the needs of its citizens, to set up programs for every need someone may have. They believe the government should tax the rich in order to pay for the needs of the poor.

If my basic presumptions are correct, then here is the answer. Conservatives believe someone should do something and they are someone. Liberals believe the government should do something, and since they are not the government, they don't need to do anything.

Because of Communism

This is very simple; Liberalism, Progressivism and Socialism are all forms of Communism. At the foundation of each is the government being in control of the people.

The foundation of the United States is limited government, with individual responsibility. The division of government between federal, state and local levels were designed specifically to avoid total governmental control over individuals. *"of the people by the people for the people"*

If you look closely at the premise for all socialist candidates, virtually every plan they have is to help someone, to provide something to someone, to give away money or services. There are only two catches; first you must give them power and authority over you. Second you must give them your money so they can help the people they believe need help. This type of candidate assumes you and people like you cannot take care of yourself without the government. If you are one of the people who has enough money to take care of yourself: then you have more than you need, so the government should tax you more in order to give better care to the people who cannot care for them selves.

Listen closely to the candidates and you will see for yourself that what I am saying is correct. If you are truly one of the people who need the government to provide for you, vote Liberal/Communist.

Because of Criminals

We have a group of people in this country who have decided, for whatever reason, to not play by the rules. They do not want to get a job, pay their bills, and raise their children like most of us do. They prefer to steal, sell drugs or find some other way to get out of honest work that the rest of us do. We also have a large number of people who are violent. They rape, murder, or in other ways destroy lives.

Our criminal justice system does a poor job in protecting us. The police can catch the bad guys and get them to court. In many cases we put them in jail. Then we give them early parole and turn them out on the society they could not live in before. The story is that we do not have enough room in our prisons for all of the criminals, so we cannot keep them locked up for the full term of their sentence.

Here is the bad part: when you look into crimes that are committed in the U.S. today, a very high percentage are committed by people who should still be in prison. How many times do you hear on the local news of someone on parole committing the same type of crime they were convicted of before? If they were still in jail where they belong, someone would still be alive, or have not been raped or a child would not have been molested, if we had just kept them in jail for the whole sentence.

I know, at some point most of them have to get out of jail. When they do, we run the same risk of them committing more crimes. Remember, if they stay in jail for the full five or ten years that's five or ten years we are that much safer.

More prisons to keep the bad guys away from my family is one of the few reasons I would gladly pay more taxes.

Because of Diversity

We hear about the value of diversity in the workplace, schools and our neighborhoods. Notably the diversity that is referred to is not in the world of ideas. It requires individuals of different skin color, as if the color of your skin is the deciding factor in developing your beliefs. Whereas I can appreciate the value of differing thoughts to either justify mine or bring correction to my thought process, the federal government should not be in the business of implementing diversity based on skin color or religious belief.

When the federal government makes policy or implements laws it should only recognize only two types of people: American citizens and everyone else. The government of this country has the responsibility to take care of its citizens. In no circumstance should one group of Americans receive benefit or detriment under the law. The laws and policies of our country should apply equally to men and women, blacks and whites, Jews and Gentiles and every variation of each category. We would never have policies that noticed a difference between Americans who are descendants from Germany and the ones from France. Why then would our policies recognize a difference between descendants of Africa and descendants of South America?

If you are an American citizen you have an equal share in the inheritance of freedom, and the privileges and responsibilities that go with being an American citizen. This is yours without any governmental program; don't let politicians tell you they will give you what you deserve if you elect them. It's yours already.

Diversity is not a good thing if one group of Americans has to surrender to another group of Americans their liberties or equality.

"We hold these truths to be self-evident, that all men are created equal, that they are endowed by their Creator with certain unalienable Rights, that among these are life, liberty and the pursuit of happiness. "

Because of Evil

"All evil needs to persist, is for good men to do nothing"

I don't know who the original author of this is, but it's true. The point is not to let evil continue unchecked. The most vocal part of our society are those who would remove all morality, standards of truth and personal responsibility.

They vote, do you?

Evil is not always bad people doing bad things, sometimes its good people doing nothing.

Because of Gun Control

Many of the liberal politicians are promoting some kind of federal gun control. They blame the high level of crime, including murders and gang violence on guns. They also blame the gun industry for making guns that work.

Blaming guns for murders is like blaming the filing cabinet at work for loosing files. The filing cabinet is an inanimate object, subject to proper use by people. Guns are the same, a gun has never picked itself up, gone to a liquor store, and shot the cashier. It was the bad guy who did.

Are the liberal politicians who advocate more gun control so stupid they cannot understand it's the people, not the guns? I don't think so. For some inexplicable reason they do not want to promote punishment for the criminals who do the crimes. The answer to gun violence is not getting rid of guns; it's getting rid of criminals.

Please understand that the criminals are not going to follow any new gun control law. The law-abiding citizens are the only ones who will follow the new laws. If they are not currently breaking the laws, why should we take their guns away? We shouldn't.

I remember hearing about Australia having their murder rate go through the roof after they outlawed private gun ownership. The bad guys did not turn in their guns, only the good guys.

Don't let the liberal politicians get away with blaming the filing cabinet any more.

Because of Liberty

There is a small town in Arkansas about five miles from the Mississippi River where the county court house has an inscription over the entrance that reads, "Obedience to the law is liberty". This works every time. Let me give you some examples, if you are driving on the highway at a speed of 75 miles per hour in a 55 miles per hour zone. What happens when you see a police officer? Your foot slams on the break; your heart races and your hands shake as you zoom by. How much liberty do you feel? If you drove by the officer at 54 mph how much liberty would you feel?

This also works with your daily life. When I was a small boy I was taught the Ten Commandments were to protect me. In my youth I did not understand, but as I matured and had some life experiences I began to understand. Here is one example of my personal liberty: The other day my family and I were driving down the street when we saw a roadside monument of crosses. My daughter asked what they were for, and as my wife explained to her it was for AIDS awareness, I was strangely comforted. I was comforted because I have no fear of contracting AIDS. You see, I'm living faithfully to my wife and do not use intravenous drugs. By doing the right things I am safe from infection. By being obedient to the Commandment that said do not commit adultery; I have liberty, liberty from AIDS and all other sexually transmitted diseases. If ever I need blood during surgery I hope and pray the blood supply is safe.

If you live your life doing the right things, the right things will happen. If you do the wrong things, the wrong things will happen. If you would like to live in liberty, try being obedient to the laws designed to protect you.

Because of Marriage

Marriage is between a man and a woman.

Homosexual relationships should not be given the validity of true marriage. True marriage was originally ordained by God, and has been the social tradition for over 6000 years. One man, one woman as husband and wife, mother and father, raising their children. This is not optional, two mothers or two fathers is a perversion of the family, and our government should never give homosexual relationships validity.

If they choose to live what is politely called an alternative lifestyle, that's fine. Please understand that it is called alternative because it is not the normal lifestyle of human beings.

Our government should not be in the business of legitimizing alternative life styles. Why is it illegal for a man to have more than one wife? Why is a man having an affair with a woman, or man other than his wife grounds for divorce? Should we give them alternative lifestyle status also? No.

Our federal government should not have laws that discriminate against what consenting adults do with each other in private. It also should not support alternatives to normal behavior.

Because of Maturity

Nobody is born mature; we all have to grow into it. Using my own children as an example, when they were first born they required food from their mother's body. Then they were given a bottle, then baby cereal. When their teeth came in we started to give them solid food, but it was cut in very small pieces. At some point my wife and I taught our children to cut their own food. The oldest now knows how to cook when he is hungry; the other two are working towards cooking. The next step will be for our children to be capable of earning the money to buy their own food. The final step is the ability to buy food for themselves and their children, raising their children to maturity. This is the way we have learned from the beginning of time.

Why then do liberal social programs not require anyone to grow to maturity? They will give the food away without teaching anyone how to go to the next step. If we did not teach our children how to get their own food what would happen to them? They would be at the mercy of others. Is that why the liberals don't want the people on social programs to become self-sufficient? That way the people are dependent on the politicians.

If the politicians make a large enough group of people dependent on them, they will ensure power for themselves virtually forever. I say we support politicians that will help the least among us grow to maturity. That is definitely not the Liberal Democrats.

Because of National Security

A basic premise of the Republican Party is a strong military: so strong and advanced technologically that no one in the world would ever stand a chance of defeating us on the battlefield. I believe this is the best chance we have in never being attacked on our own soil by any country. Peace through strength works.

In order for it to work everyone must believe we are willing to use the military to defend ourselves. This sometimes means using the military to reinforce that understanding.

Traditionally the Democrats reduce spending on the military in order to spend on social programs. This dramatically reduces our national security.

One thing that cannot be debated is that we will never have freedom without security.

Because of our Rights

I hear a lot of people talking about all the rights they have. The rights they have to live the lifestyle they choose the way they choose. The right to do what they want when they want, and nobody should say anything about what they choose to do.

I have no problem with Americans exercising their rights. The issue I have is the lack of understanding of "rights." Every right comes with an equal portion of responsibility. One of the biggest problems in this country's society today is the lack of understanding of responsibilities.

You have the right to drive a car. First you are responsible for obtaining a driver's license. Then you are responsible for buying a car. Next you must get auto insurance. Then you get to put the car on the road. Now you have the responsibility to obey the laws of the road. The next consideration is the vehicle itself. You are responsible for the proper maintenance of the vehicle. When you are driving, you are responsible for everything that happens in the car and to the car.

Remember the greater the right, the greater the responsibility. If you choose to exercise the rights you have, you must accept the responsibilities.

Because of Pornography

In the 2000 presidential election, the states where Al Gore received the most votes also spent the most on pornography.

The states where George W. Bush received the most votes, spent the least on pornography.

What does this mean? I am not sure. But it is very interesting information.

Who are you supporting?

Because of Racism

Because of the Democrats' social agenda, every one of us is forced to be constantly aware of our race, and everyone else's. What do I mean? I'll tell you what I mean.

My ancestry goes like this, English, Irish, Scottish, Welsh, German and Iroquois. I am descended from German Royalty; my maternal ancestors are from the house Stuart in England. All of my ancestry has been reduced down to "WHITE" the color of my skin. As if the color of my skin makes any difference as to whether I can do the job I am applying for, or anything else I would ever fill out a form for.

I have two cousins whose father is of African descent; when they fill out forms they are forced to check a block that says "BLACK" or "AFRICAN AMERICAN," as if that makes any difference or defines whom they are. They are my cousins; they lived on the same street and went to the same schools as I did. They have the same grandparents as do I, yet the social engineers have put them in a box, a different box then I am in. Why? Why can both my cousins and I not just be Americans? We all came from somewhere, we all have a story to tell, some sad, some not so sad. Why does the story define who we are? My royal blood does me no good today, as it shouldn't.

What should matter is how I live my life; do I take care of my wife and my children? Am I a productive member of society? Do I obey the laws of the land?

When we put everyone in a box on a form and try to define them by the color of their skin, that is racism at its most basic. As long as the government practices racism we can never remove racism from the hearts and minds of the average person on the street.

We are all so much more than a box on a form. The only question the federal government should ask is:

Are you a U.S. Citizen?

Because of Rich People

I know a family that lives in the middle of the country who the Democrats say is rich. When they sent their oldest son to college two years ago they filled out all the forms for federal aid. According to the federal government this family of five should be able to spend over $11,000.00 per year to pay for college. This amazed me. I know how much the family's income is and the idea that they have an extra $1,000.00 per month lying around is absurd.

Here is what rich looks like to the liberal Democrats. This family has one income, the father's, and the mother stays home to rear the children. This is an outline of the family's income.

Gross Income, $82,719.07   Federal taxes, $6,511.07
Social Security $4,933.37   Medicare tax $1,153.77
State tax $3,555.28   Medical insurance $2,772.12
Dental Insurance $419.12   Vision $210.08
401K Savings $1,774.14
Which leaves $61,390.12 or $5,115.84 per month.

According to the federal government this family should be able to spend about 18% of its total take-home income on a college education for one of their children, because they are rich.

This family did get a tax cut from George W. Bush, so we know they are rich according to the liberal Democrats.

I believe this family is smack in the middle of the middle class. They are not rich; they are not poor. They have never bought a brand new car. They take the children to a movie from time to time and family vacations consist going to see family members who live cross-country. Not Disney Land, because it cost too much.

When you hear the liberal Democrats complain about tax cuts for the rich you will never hear them say what rich is. This family is whom they are talking about. This rich family is very happy to have their tax cut so they can take care of themselves better.

Because of Stupidity

Stupidity is different from ignorance, the cure for ignorance is information, and stupidity is forever.

Some people simply do not understand this; others cannot understand the information when they get it.

The people who upset me are the ones who understand the information but twist it to meet whatever agenda they have. They count on us to be stupid.

Because of Taxes

Yes, the federal, state and local governments need to tax us, their citizens. As a general rule, republicans believe in taxing at a level which allows the government to pay for the military, the day-to-day expenses of operation, federal disaster relief, to provide assistance to other countries whose governments believe in the same fundamental right and responsibilities of a free society. To provide educational assistance and short-term welfare for the few who do not yet have the skills to survive in this world on their own. Beyond that, Republicans believe in a market-based economy, where companies who provide quality products and services will be profitable. Individuals who work harder, smarter or longer will command a higher salary. And we believe that the men and women who earn the money should be allowed to decide how to spend the money.

Democrats, in general, believe that it is their job to dictate how the money is spent and who does the spending. They believe that it is their right and obligation to take from the men and women who make too much (in their opinion) and give it to those who make too little. This is called re-distribution of wealth. The idea is to not let the gap between the rich and the poor become too large. A good example of this is what has become known as the death tax. Understand that most republicans agree that it should be completely eliminated. When a man or woman dies and leaves a great deal of money for their children or other family members, the federal government taxes the cash and value of property of the inheritance up to 50%. Now understand the income taxes have already been paid when the money was originally earned. Also property taxes were paid annually, and in some cases, personal property taxes were paid to state and local governments. So what good reason do the Democrats give for continuing this double taxation? The government needs the money. If they cannot tax the inheritance of the rich they will lose millions every year. This is the most obvious case of wealth re-distribution I can find. Why? Because what will the Democratic politicians do with the money? Feed the poor, give it to schools, pay for new roads, give it to farmers to grow crops that are not profitable or to not grow crops at all, promote the policies of like-minded individuals. Please notice that at no point will the men and women who the money was taken from benefit from it. Why should we tax someone who has the universal experience of dying? We should not. Over the years thousands of family farms have been destroyed by taxes. Companies have been sold off or closed down to pay the death taxes, and a lifetime of hard work is destroyed. Think about it for a minute, how would you feel if your work was destroyed? How would you feel if you worked and saved your whole life to build a good life for your children, and the government came in and took by force, half of everything you built for your children? When asked why, the answer is that we need it more than your children do. We have poor people who need money, food, a home and health care. So we are going to take half of your life's work and give it to people who we think deserve a better life. Just the thought of that makes me mad enough to fight. Yes, I would fight anyone who steals from my children. Wait a minute, its not called stealing if the government does it. It's called taxes. That does not make me feel any better about it. How about you? Everyone should pay their fair share of operating the government. If you make more money you will be asked to pay more, if you make less you will be asked to pay less or nothing. And that is just a fact of life, yet understand it has never been the mission of our federal government to play Robin Hood, stealing from the rich and giving to the poor. It is the mission of the government to provide an even playing field for each individual to use their God-given talents in pursuit of life, liberty, and personal happiness.

Because of the Bill of Rights

The Bill of Rights contains the first 10 Amendments to the Constitution. The Bill of Rights was approved by all states in 1791, three years after the constitution was approved. The Bill of Rights outlines basic liberties of the people, which the government cannot violate.

#1 Congress shall make no law respecting the establishment of religion, or prohibiting the free exercise thereof; or abridging the freedom of speech, or of the press; or the rights of the people peaceably to assemble, and to petition the government for a redress of grievances.

To the best of my knowledge the congress has never attempted to establish religion, or prohibit the free exercise there of. The courts have. We hear all the time about the "separation of church and state." There is no such thing in the Declaration of Independence, the Constitution, or the Bill of Rights. The courts have been removing any reference to God or religion from all public buildings and property based on something that does not exist.

They have been prohibiting the free exercise of religion every time they remove the Ten Commandments, forbid a nativity scene on public property and even when my daughter's first grade teacher told her not to talk about Jesus in our public school.

Remember the first Amendment guarantees the free exercise of religion, with out listing any restrictions as to places that it could not be practiced or, prohibiting the government from practicing their religion in public. As long as no government entities try to force anyone to worship, everyone is constitutionally protected to practice religion anywhere.

Because of the Death Penalty

Generally speaking, the Republicans believe in the proper application of the death penalty. The Democrats don't.

I believe it is the responsibility of the government to protect the innocent and to punish the guilty. The appropriate Punishment for murder is the death penalty.

Properly applied, the death penalty not only is a punishment, it is also a deterrent. If the sentence of death is implemented in a timely fashion, then criminals will respect it. When murderers can live in jail for 20 or 25 years with out applying the death penalty, what level of deterrent is that? None.

Some people will tell you that a good reason to eliminate the death penalty is to protect innocent people from it. I do not ever want to have an innocent person put to death. This argument is a great argument for reforming our courts, not for eliminating the death penalty.

The death penalty is not the problem; the criminals are the problem. I would prefer our political leaders protect the law-abiding citizens from the criminals, not the criminals, from the law.

Because of the Democrats Sales Strategy

I remember back in the early 1990's being trained a sales tactic that was new to me but had been around for years. The instructor called it dragging the customer over broken glass.

This is the sales strategy the Democratic politician's use on a daily basis. Here is how it works. You identify a small problem or annoyance that your prospect has. Then you magnify it to an extreme. The epitome of making a mountain out of a molehill. You hit home on how munch pain it is causing the prospect or heighten their fear to almost panic mode. The next part is warning the solution is going to cost, really cost. But it will be worth it to stop the pain or remove the fear. Then you provide the answer. Now this sales tactic works very well because you only identify problems you have answers for. Or at lest an answer the prospect will buy.

Understand that all buying decisions are made emotional and justified by logic. Watch the Democrats play Chicken Little as they scream the sky is falling, the sky is falling. Then sell you a net to go under the apple tree.

As you are dragged over the broken glass by the politicians who list everything that is wrong with the greatest nation ever conceived on this planet, remember the close is coming when they ask you to sign on the dotted line.

The democrats have paid good attention in their sales training. I hope you are paying attention too. Because it's going to cost, it's going to cost a lot.

Because of the Economy

It's the economy stupid! Yes, the economy is very important. For years we have said that it's the president's economy. The Carter economy, the Regan economy, the Bush economy, the Clinton economy, the Bush economy. If the economy is good the president at the time takes credit for it, if it's bad the opponents of the president place the blame on the president.

Understand that the president of the United States does not drive the economy. The president can harm the economy much more easily, than help it. We are the economy; we buy things and drive the economy. The more money we have, the more things we buy. If I have a job and earn more money than I need for the bare essentials, I can afford to take my family out to dinner, go on a vacation, buy a bigger house, a new car, and my children can have two or three new pair of shoes for school instead of just one. The key to this whole thing is how much money I get to take home out of my paycheck. When I control my money I put it into the economy which helps the companies I buy from. When the companies I buy from sell more stuff, they need to hire more employees. When they hire more employees more people have jobs, when more people have jobs more people have money to buy more things and so on.

Now how is it that the president can do more harm than good? That's easy: they can take the money away from the people who earn it and out of the economy.

Look back at the last 25 years, Carter's economy was in big trouble, interest rates were through the roof, manufacturing was not. Reagan came in and dramatically reduced the tax burden on companies and individuals. The result? Our economy steadily built up for the next 18 years. Bill Clinton took credit for the great economy, but his tax increases slowed down the economy to the point that we sank into a recession starting in 1999. George W. Bush had to deal with the problem. What was the answer? Tax cuts to give the money back to the people who earned it. Let them use the money to buy stuff to take care of their families.

What happened? By the end of 2003 the economy came back strong.

Democrats raise your taxes; Republicans lower your taxes.

You make the decision........

Because of the Family Farm

The family farm in this country is in danger. We started losing family farms over a hundred years ago. Sometimes the children of farmers just did not want to farm for a living. Sometimes the farms were wiped out by drought, flood or other natural disaster. If the family did not have the money to start over the bank got the farm. Our own government distorted many family farms with the inheritance tax. When the old man who farmed his whole life died, his children had to pay up to 50% of the value of the farm to the government. Farming is not the kind of business where the family has a lot of cash in the bank. All the value is in the land and equipment. If the value of the farm was a million dollars, the children had to pay 50% to the government; they were forced to sell the farm to pay the taxes. This is one of the worst things our government has ever done.

The federal government has put together many, many programs for farmers. Hundreds of billions of dollars have been spent on farm subsidies. But still small farmers go out of business every year. I guess they did not get the money. When you look at the list of companies that received the money, a tremendous amount goes to multi-million dollar companies. Why does a multi-million dollar company need government subsidies?

The people who raise our food on farms and ranches should not be taxed and then told if they fit into a specific program then the government will help them. If you could grow sugar cane instead of corn the government would help.

I have to admit I am not big on farm subsidies, I'm OK with disaster coverage, but not with paying farmers to grow pine trees instead of food. What I would like to see is something that would remove all taxes from the family farm. Not Archer Daniel's Midlan, but the family farm. I could get behind some kind of low interest loans that would be guaranteed by the FED so the banks would not foreclose on the farms. Something that actually helps the family farm.

I know none of this seems to follow my otherwise harsh beliefs, but the family farm is too important to this country and the world. Plus I personally know some former family farmers who had to get out of the business. The subsidies did not get to them but the taxes did.

Because of the Golden Rule

Most of us are familiar with the paraphrased biblical version, "Do unto others as you want them to do to you." That's not the one I refer to at this point. The Golden Rule I'm talking about is **"He who has the gold makes the rules."** This version affects us more than we know; let's take a look at how often it really affects our lives.

First, my father and mother controlled the money when I was growing up. I'll give you one guess as to who made the rules in the house. That's right, they did. In my late teens I worked for a small company, the owner worked longer hours and harder during those hours than anybody else. Yes, you are on the right track, he made the rules. As a Young adult I moved out of my parents' home, I earned the gold at this point; guess who made the rules in that apartment? You're right, I did. Even when my parents came over they followed my rules in my home. I had the gold, I made the rules. We could go on and on with example after example, but I think you are getting the idea. Let's look at how this affects whom you should vote for.

When we vote for people who will set policy for our Country we give them authority to tax us. With the taxes they take out of our paychecks they run the government and set up "Social Programs." The programs that are currently in place would take up this whole book, so we will not list all of them. Let's look at how when the government takes the gold from us we surrender our ability to make the rules for our lives and give it to the government.

I will start with the most expensive program that affects everyone who has a job. Social Security: the federal government forcibly takes 12% of your first $87,000.00 of income. Yes, the number is 12.4%: you see 6.2% come out of your check stub, the other 6.2% is paid to the government on your behalf by your company.

They are giving it to the government so they cannot afford to give it to you. This money is taken from you over your entire life, your money that you have no control over. The government is making the rules. They have the gold you earned; now they tell you when you can get it back. You would like to retire at age 60, which is fine, but you will not receive your full benefits because the government now has the gold, and they get to make the rules. We have had several politicians who want to raise the age at which you can start getting your own money back. They have your gold: they get to make the rules on when you get your money back, and how much they will give you, how often and even if you are allowed to earn more money. Did you know when you are retired and the government is giving you back the money that they took from you over the last 40 plus years, they will limit how much you can earn? If you find something you want to do during your retirement the government will stop sending you your own money if you get paid more than what they think you should be allowed. Remember they have your gold they make the rules.

Because of the Main Stream

I hear a lot of talk about Mainstream America, only I do not recognize the stream they are describing. When I look at who is talking about mainstream America I understand why I do not recognize what they are describing. It's because they are normally Liberal Democrats, and they don't live in the same stream as most Americans.

Let me describe what I believe to be Main Stream America. The stream is very wide and colorful, filled with families raising their children. Most of the families go to church on Sunday and try to practice what they learned the rest of the week. Main Stream Americans go to work, send their children to school and say <u>Under God</u> during the pledge of allegiance. In this stream we know not every one lives by the normal standards. There are homosexuals in the stream, but they don't throw their lifestyle in anyone's face. We know abortions happen, but are kept quiet because they know what they did was wrong. Main Stream Americans still have moral standards about sex and money. The stream cuts down trees for wood and paper but plants even more than they cut down. They like good gas mileage but prefer safety for their children. They thank God and the people who serve for our military. They treat you with respect even when you are wrong. They do want the Ten Commandments in public places and like nativity scenes at Christmas. Main Stream America does not want to build a wall around our country to keep everyone out or leave the door open to let everyone in. They believe it's ok for our government to kill terrorists wherever they are found. The main stream pays their taxes even though they are too high. They vote more often than they don't.

If you would like to see Mainstream America go to the shopping mall, the grocery store, the ball field, high school gymnasiums. Go anywhere mothers and fathers take their children. Go to places

you could tell your mother you went with out being embarrassed.
There you will find Mainstream America.

Because of the Minimum Wage

The minimum wage is set up as the lowest wage that can be paid for time at work. This is designed for low-skill jobs like the dishwasher at a restaurant, the cashier for fast food, the person who stocks the shelves at the grocery store or collects the shopping carts jobs that require no education or training, the kind of job you work while your are in high school or college. They are not designed for anyone who is supporting a family, or even responsible for completely supporting themselves. Minimum wage is not set up for a person to be able to buy a home, new car or feed a family. The way you earn more than minimum wage is by becoming more valuable to the market place. You must have the ability to complete complex tasks that require training. Either start at the bottom and work your way up or attend a trade school or college.

If we follow the lead of the liberals who believe minimum wage should be set high enough to support a family of four we will be in big trouble. We would need to double the minimum wage in order to be above the poverty level. How much will a Big Mac cost if we pay $15.00 per hour to have someone make it?

What would happen to all the people who have worked hard to get to the point of earning $15.00 per hour? The cost of everything would go up because the companies who provide products and services would have to raise prices in order to pay the new minimum wage. Now the money they earn will buy less than it did before. Essentially they have been reduced to minimum wage employees again. The people who do not know how to do anything will be paid $15.00 per hour, but if the price of everything goes up they still will not be able to support a family. Guess what, you will need to pay more for everything, too. That means your money will buy less; this is the same as taking a pay cut.

What makes more sense? Everyone in the country taking a pay cut in order to raise the minimum wage or expecting everyone to learn a trade of some kind so they can earn a living for themselves?

Because of the Pledge of Allegiance

I pledge allegiance to the Flag of the United States of America,
*to the republic for which it stands, one nation **under God**,*
indivisible with liberty and justice for all.

The God of Abraham, Isaac and Jacob have been at the very foundation of our country from before we fought and won our independence. The Judeo Christian values of the colonists had been in affect for over four hundred years. In the early 1960's we, as a God-fearing nation, started to surrender our values to a small number of atheists. As we remove God from our institutions in this country we can track the decline in each institution. Look at our schools, they are an absolute disaster. In the 1950's chewing gum and talking in class were some of the big offenses. Teenage pregnancy was so low that schools did not bother to track the percentages. One every few years was easy to keep track of

It is much safer **under God** than without God.

Do not let the ungodly take any more away.

Because of the Right-Wing Conspiracy

In listening to the liberal politicians complain about the Vast Right-Wing Conspiracy, I think I may be a part of it. When they complain about the 10 Commandment in courts, I want them there. When they complain about the tax cuts, I am thankful for mine. Every time they complain about the vast right wing conspiracy, I agree with the conspirators. None of them called me about anything, so maybe it's not a conspiracy, just a bunch of people who are smarter than the average bear.

Every time the people on the left complain about the people on the right, they are simply disagreeing with individuals of an opposing view. Why would they call it a conspiracy? Because they cannot win the argument with facts, so they have to resort to name calling, just like the children on the playground at my son's school. That is exactly how children behave when they do not have the knowledge or skill to win the argument, they start calling names.

Look at the people who are doing the name-calling and the people who are being called names. I would prefer to be considered a member of the Vast Right-Wing Conspiracy rather than a member of the name callers. How about you?

Because of the Special Interests Groups

Because the Democratic Party is the party of special interests. Virtually every group that wants something aligns themselves with the Democrats, partly because the Democratic Party promises to give them things.

It's no secret that lots of business owners support traditional Republican candidates. The first reason I can think of for this is that the traditional Republican candidate runs on a platform of limited government. This means less regulation on most companies and lower taxes. Of course both lead to more profitable companies. Also most Americans who worship God vote conservatively because the conservative agenda matches very closely to the Bible.

When I say the Democratic Party is the party of special interests I'm talking about the vast number of special interest groups aligned with the Democratic Party. Let's see how many we can name. The vast number of workers unions, teachers unions, autoworkers and so on Gay rights groups, abortion rights groups, The National Organization of Women, the NAACP, and Latino Organizations. Environmentalist Groups like E.L.F whose members act like terrorists, burning SUV dealerships and new homes being built in the mountains. Others who spike trees so loggers will be hurt or maimed when they do their jobs P.E.T.A. who has gone so far overboard we have no way of bringing them back. The atheists who want God out of our government, the liberal movie companies who want less morality holding them back. The Peace movement groups who don't believe anything are worth fighting for. We could go on, but I think you get the idea.

What I don't understand is, what do the unions and homosexual groups have in common? Why would good Catholic Latinos vote for pro-abortion liberals? What does the NAACP have in conmen with P.E.T.A? Each group by it's self is too small to accomplish anything. So if they band to gather they can increase their influence by saying, if you vote for my stuff I will vote for yours.

So who is really the party of special interests?

Because of Tolerance

The liberal politicians continue to ask all conservatives to be tolerant. So I decided to find out what it was exactly they wanted from me. I looked it up. According to the Merriam-Webster Dictionary, the definition of tolerance is #1 Capacity to endure pain or hard ship. I don't think that they expect me to endure pain so they can have what they want. Let's look at #2 Sympathy or indulgence for beliefs or practices differing from or conflicting with one's own. This must be what they are asking for, but wait a minute. They don't do this, do they? If you exercise your religious beliefs and say that homosexuality is bad, they call you names like "Homophobe". If you speak out that abortion is killing the baby, you are trampling on a woman's constitutional right to choose what to do with her own body, and you are not being tolerant. Definition #2 does not say I have to agree with them, just put up with them. So that cannot be what they are asking. Let's look at definition #4 The capacity of the body to endure or become less responsive to a substance or physiological insult with repeated use or exposure. This sounds like what they are looking for. That explains why they use the insults and name-call so much. It also explains why every time someone disagrees with them they scream about tolerance. They want us to become less responsive to what they do and say, so they have no challengers to the direction they are trying to steer this Country in.

This is the same idea as boiling a frog. If you throw a frog into a pot of boiling water he will jump out so fast he may not even get warm. But if you place the same frog in room temperature water he will be comfortable and stay. You can then turn up the temperature until he starts to become uncomfortable and wiggle around. Wait for some time until he becomes comfortable with his new surroundings. Now that he is happy staying in this temperature of water, and you can turn up the heat some more, repeating until the water boils. This process works every time, the frog stays in the water until he is boiled and ready to eat.

I will not be the frog; I can live up to the expectations of #2 but will not put up with #4.

How about you?

Because of World Peace

I was in a coffee shop back in the late 1980's and had the opportunity to overhear a conversation between some young college students and an old W.W.II Vet. The students had obviously been subject to the liberal ranting of some professors at the local college. They were trying to convince the old man that war should never be an option. We should try to negotiate our differences with other countries. If necessary we should change our country's polices in order to avoid a war. They tried to explain to this member of the greatest generation, how we could find out why countries did not like us then we could find some middle ground. If we had some middle ground we would never have to go to war. The old vet was becoming frustrated with the lack of understanding the college students demonstrated.

He tried to explain we would never have world peace in our lifetime, and how political and religious differences would always divide countries. Also he tried to explain that bad people would take over small countries and mistreat their people. He attempted to explain communism to the young men, but they interrupted him, saying communism is not all bad. At that point the old vet decided to surrender the battle leaving the young men with their ignorance. After he finished his cup of coffee, the old man left them with this thought.

The only way to have world peace is to kill all of the bad people in the world. The hard part is getting everyone to agree on who the bad people are.

It's is a shame that it takes 60 or 70 years of experience to have the kind of wisdom that old vet had. But since it does, lets all find an old vet and ask the questions we desperately need answered.

I believe he's right. We will not have world peace in our generation. The best we can hope for is security for our people.

Because Religious People Cannot Vote for Democrats.

Why, you ask? Well, I guess they can vote for Democrats, but they must do so at the risk of violating the will of God. Now most Americans claim to worship the God of the Bible. But even the people in this country who worship other gods cannot vote for candidates who support homosexuals having special rights under the law. They cannot support candidates who support abortions.

I am not aware of any religion, which allows for the killing of unborn children or allows for homosexual behavior. So when a person who claims to be religious votes for a candidate whose political positions go against their religion, what are they doing? They are going against their God, or at least ignoring their God.

How can you have any respect for a person who will go against their God for political reasons? What about the candidates who claim to be religious yet support the same things? If they will disregard what their God says when they support policies, when else will they disregard him? If politicians will kick God out of their lives from Monday through Saturday, what good is their religion?

__Because Small Business is Good__

Small business is good for America; the entrepreneurial sprit is one of the strongest reasons this country has been successful. Most of the life changing inventions of the past 200 years has come from individuals with small businesses. Life-changing inventions such as the telegraph, telephone, electricity, broadcast radio, television, the automobile assembly line, the photocopier, desktop computers and so on.

How did the small business that invented these products benefit the country? General Electric, Bell Telephone, AT&T, Ford, Xerox, ABC, NBC, CBS and so on. They are some of the financial giants in our country today. (See because big business is good)

Small business also employs about 50% of the non-governmental employees in the county.

Small business is typically community-oriented; they advertise by sponsoring local sports teams. They get involved with the local schools. Local charities and churches go to the successful small business owners for help with outreach programs. They often help high school and college students with summer jobs.

Small business offers some of the best service to its customers. They know you by name and really care that you come back again.

I have a tremendous respect for every small business owner. The amount of work that is required and risk they take would crush most individuals today.

Because the Democrats are on the Wrong Side of Good and Bad

You read the title and said to yourself that good people are on the side of good and bad people are on the side of bad, not believing that good people who are Democrats are on the side of bad.

At its foundation the Democratic Party is pro-choice and anti-death penalty, RIGHT?

At the foundation of the Republican Party you find pro-life and support for the death penalty, RIGHT?

Good people with the most basic foundation of morality would all agree that the innocent should be protected and the guilty punished. You would agree with that, and so do I. Why then does the Democratic party promote the killing of our most innocent (unborn children) and appose the death penalty for the guilty?

Because their moral foundation is askew, it takes someone with a strong foundation to stand up and proclaim right and wrong.

I will do it now; our laws should protect the innocent and punish the guilty.

Yes, the death penalty is moral when applied to the worst criminals, specifically murderers and those who kill someone while they are committing a crime.

Because the Democrat Leaders will turn the war in Iraq in to Vietnam.

First you need to understand we did not lose in Vietnam because we did not have the military strength, or because we could not figure out how to use our military to win. We lost because we did not have the political will to win.

Every Democratic leader who steps up to a microphone wants out of Iraq one way or another. They either did not want to go in, or want to leave before we are finished rebuilding, or don't wont to spend the money to do the job right.

If we leave for any reason before we have accomplished everything that needs to be done, no matter what excuse we use, the terrorists will have won. If they think they ran us out because of suicide bombings or any other terrorist tactics they may come up with. They will continue to use those tactics everywhere in the world including, Los Angeles, Chicago, Atlanta, or even your town.

The worst of the worst are the ones who say we need to turn over authority to the United Nations. This will do nothing but subject the Iraqi people and us to the total incompetence of the Security Council. Yes, I did mean to say incompetence. Any group who puts together ten, twelve, fifteen or more resolutions without enforcing even one is incompetent. If you raised your children that way they would not behave any better than Sodom did. When my father said stop whatever it was I was doing "or else". He meant the "or else" and he followed through with the "or else". Even a small boy is smart enough to figure out whether the parent will follow through with the "or else" or not.

The Iraq war will cost too much money, too many lives and take too long. Even with the high costs, we and the rest of the world will be better off for it. Going forward, all countries and terrorist organizations will know when the American President says "or else" he means it and will follow through with it. This simple understanding will put a stop to many, many attract before they ever start. And this will help cut the cost in money and lives.

Do not let the politicians put us and the rest of the world at the mercy of the terrorists. They have no mercy.

Because the Devil is Working Hard in America.

I know when most of your read the title of this section you thought about all kinds of bad things. The drug dealers, the gangs who keep shooting each other in our streets, the rapists, murders and child molesters. But they are not who I am talking about. The people who are doing the Devil's work that voting republican will help stop, are people like the ACLU. The people who are going to court to remove God from every aspect of our lives. The people who believe " under God" should be removed from the pledge of allegiance because one atheist does not wont his child to say it in school. Keeping every one from saying "under God."

Let me ask you this, who is it that would like to remove God and morality from our county? Is it God, or is it Satan? Even if the people who are doing the work of Satan, are not Satan worshipers, or have intent of helping him, they are doing his work for him and he loves it.

Some politicians are helping the work of Satan by supporting the organizations that are trying to remove God from this country. If you are on God's side in this world stop voting for people who are helping the Devil.

Because the Liberal Media Misquotes God

This misquotation is absolutely done with full knowledge and purpose. The writers who put the movies and television shows together do a tremendous amount of research for accuracy. Why then do they continually misquote God? They do it on purpose in order to mislead the general public.

Following are two primary examples of the liberal media's misquoting God. First we have all heard this one from the 10 commandments. "Thou shall not kill." This is not in the Ten Commandments. The Commandment is "Thou shall not murder." Big difference in murder and kill, in war you kill your enemy on the battlefield. Murder is the premeditated killing of an innocent person. The second example is that "money is the root of all evil". Not in the Bible, the quote is "The <u>love</u> of money is the root of all evil". Again a big difference.

I challenge each of you who are not already familiar with this information to read the Bible.

Now the translation you read may vary some from what I have listed above, but the intent will not. When the media changes the words they change the intent, that's where the evil is.

Because There is a Right and Proper way to live Your Life

In today's society many people choose an alternative life style. Little Johnny has two Mommies and Suzie has two Daddies. Uncle John and his friend Jack are coming over for dinner. Or we have parents who do not get married but have several children with different partners. The standard answer from a vast majority of those who choose to live an alternative lifestyle is. "Don't judge me." It's my life and I can live it the way I choose to. It, after all, is not the place of the government or even society to tell me how to live my life. While I would agree that I do not want the government to be in the business of telling its citizens how to live their lives, I don't want those who live an alternative life style telling me how to raise my children. My children are being raised in a Christian home with morality that is founded in the Bible, not in the changing opinions of society, and understanding that the right thing is always right and the wrong thing is always wrong. The idea that right and wrong is variable or a choice to be made is absolute absurd to me. For example consider a married couple who choose to live what is called a swinging lifestyle where they have multiple sex partners with the permission of their spouse. A great number of people would say that that is fine if that is what they choose to do as long as they are not hurting anyone else. My wife and I are teaching our children that that lifestyle is wrong, and they should not be associating with those who live it. When the subject of homosexuality comes up in movies or on TV, it has been explained to my children that homosexuality is not an acceptable lifestyle. Yes some people choose to live that way, and even though a great number of people choose to live that way, that does not make it the right thing to do or a reasonable alternative.

Now with that being said, I believe that everyone has the God given right to choose how they will live their life. It is not up to the government to tell them or me how I live my life. Yet, on the other hand, I will not allow people who live in defiance of what I know is right to tell me how to live my life either. They would like me to teach my children that it's ok to live the way they want, but I will not. They, in the name of tolerance, say I should teach my children to be friends with them; I will not. They may live the life they choose and I will live the life I choose. The key is neither side should ever be able to use the government to make the other side behave the way they want.

Because Tom Daschle is a Democrat

Tom Daschle worked diligently for two long years obstructing everything President George W. Bush tried to accomplish. At every turn you could see Mr. Daschle in a press conference, speaking almost apologetically while he bashed the president.

One day he disappeared; he was simply gone. I believe it had less to do with the Republican take over of the senate and more to do with the polls in his state. As it turns out, he was less popular for all of his posturing than President Bush was. He could no longer stand up proclaiming the liberal politics of his party and be re-elected. The main stream of Democratic liberalism does not run through South Dakota. His constituents believe in God and country, in that order.

Now that becoming re-elected was more important than promoting the liberal agenda, Tom Daschle was forced to leave the spotlight, and the country is better for it.

Because our Children Deserve the Best

Your children deserve the best you have to offer, not the best the government, your neighbors or even your parents have to offer. Suppose you can afford to buy three pair of new shoes for your child, and I can only afford one pair for mine. Should your child have to give my children a pair of shoes, so they both have two pairs? No, I don't thinks so. Should the government give me the money to buy my child two more pair? No, I don't think so. It is my responsibility to provide for my children the best that I can.

If I am an industrious individual and earn lots of money, my children should benefit from my work. If I am lazy and sit on my behind, my children should only benefit from my ability to provide.

Now, understand if a young man or young woman with children needs schooling and or job training, I do believe help should be offered in the form of child care, financial aid to pay for schooling, and yes, even some cash to live on. Please understand this is an investment in the individual so they can become self-sufficient. The idea of living off society can never become a lifestyle.

Remember, if the government pays for every family to live and have health care and schooling, they are getting the money from your paycheck. This means you have less to provide for your children. I do not believe the government should forcibly take from your children so they can take care of someone else's children.

The Voters Test

Should you be voting Republican or Democrat? Here is a short questionnaire that will help. Please answer the following questions from 1 to 10. 1 being never or I disagree, 5 being I sometimes or I somewhat agree, and 10 being always or I completely agree. 2, 3, 4, 6, 7, 8 and 9 are varying degrees between never and always.

1) Government is not responsible for my success or failure. ____
2) My parents were more influential to me than my schoolteachers ____
3) I did not get the last promotion at work because someone else deserved it more ____
4) God should be involved in my everyday life ____
5) I disagree with high schools dispensing birth control. ____
6) I believe at-will abortion is wrong. ____
7) I do not expect to get special treatment from the government based on my race, religion or sex. ____
8) I believe marriage is between a man and a woman only. ____
9) We should use our military against any government who helps the terrorists ____
10) The United Nations does not act in our best interests. ____
11) We are one nation under God. ____
12) Limited government is best for all. ____
13) Parents should be able to choose which school their children attend and have tax money sent to it even if it is a religious school. ____
14) It does not take a village to raise a child, it takes two parents (and grandparents are helpful.) ____
15) We should pay fewer taxes even if some people lose benefits. ____
16) Rush Limbaugh is right. ____
17) George W. Bush is better than Bill Clinton. ____
18) Hillary Clinton should never be President. ____
19) Jeb Bush looks good for 2008. ____

20) My rights in this country come with an equal amount of responsibility. _____

Total Score: _____

20 to 75	You scored low, you should vote liberal Democrat
76 to 120	You would be considered a moderate. 76-100 You will probably vote for more Democratic candidates, 101-120 more Republican.
121 to 190	Congratulations! You are a conservative, vote Republican.
191 to 200	You are nuts, see a doctor and vote Republican.

About The Author

Stuart M. Blessing uses quotes from our Constitution, Bill of Rights, the Bible, former U.S. President and Civil rights leaders to justify his political positions. He has very strong opinions and makes his case for each, clear and understandable. You do not need to possess a Doctorate in political science to enjoy this easy to read book.